Eating Green

by Sunita Apte

Consultant: Adrienne Greve, Ph.D.
Assistant Professor, City and Regional Planning Department
California Polytechnic State University, San Luis Obispo, California

BEARPORT
PUBLISHING

New York, New York

Credits

Cover and Title Page, © Otokimus/Shutterstock; 4L, © Zibedik/Shutterstock; 4R, © Ingo Wagner/dpa/Landov; 5, © Lake Fong/Bloomberg News/Landov; 6, © David R. Frazier/PhotoEdit Inc; 7, © Brian Smith/Corbis; 8, © Justin Kase Zeightz/Alamy; 9, © Grant Heilman Photography, Inc.; 10, © Bill Aron/PhotoEdit Inc.; 11, © RandFaris/Corbis/Alamy; 12, © Jonathan Nourok/PhotoEdit Inc.; 13, © Picsfive/Shutterstock; 14, © AP Images/ Kathy Willens; 15, © Ariana Lindquist/epa/Corbis; 16, © Collection7/GlowImages/Alamy; 17, © Dave Hughes/ iStockphoto; 18, © EasyEcoBlog.com; 19, © Paul Slaughter/Omni-Photo Communications; 20, © Pichugin Dmitry/Shutterstock; 21, © AP Images/Nati Harnik; 22, © Andrew Holbrooke/Corbis; 23, © Dan Snipes/Stock Connection Blue/Alamy; 24, © Michael Newman/PhotoEdit Inc.; 25T, © Grant Heilman Photography, Inc.; 25B, © Sally A. Morgan/Ecoscene/Corbis; 26, © Gideon Mendel/Corbis; 27L, © Grant Heilman Photography, Inc.; 27C, © Elena Elisseeva/Shutterstock; 27R, © Jeff Morgan/food and drink/Alamy; 28, Courtesy of the Green Restaurant Association; 29, © AP Images/Robert F. Bukaty.

Publisher: Kenn Goin
Senior Editor: Lisa Wiseman
Creative Director: Spencer Brinker
Photo Researcher: Omni-Photo Communications, Inc.

The Going Green series is printed on recycled paper.

Library of Congress Cataloging-in-Publication Data

Apte, Sunita.
    Eating green / by Sunita Apte.
        p. cm. — (Going green)
    Includes bibliographical references and index.
    ISBN-13: 978-1-59716-965-3 (library binding)
    ISBN-10: 1-59716-965-X (library binding)
    1. Sustainable agriculture—Juvenile literature. 2. Natural foods—Juvenile literature. I. Title.
    SD494.5.S86A67 2010
    630—dc22
                            2009019183

For more information, write to Bearport Publishing Company, Inc., 101 Fifth Avenue, Suite 6R, New York, New York 10003. Printed in the United States of America.

10 9 8 7 6 5 4 3 2 1

Contents

Energy for Food

Most of the food on supermarket shelves requires lots of **energy** to produce. Take ketchup, for example. It begins with tomatoes that were grown with the help of planting and harvesting machines that need a lot of energy to operate. The factory where the tomatoes were turned into ketchup used energy for cooking and for running the machines that put the finished ketchup into bottles. Then more energy was used to ship the bottles to supermarkets.

Most of this energy came from **fossil fuels** such as oil and coal that were turned into gasoline and electricity. Unfortunately, using these fuels is not **sustainable**. They are in limited supply on Earth and will eventually run out. Using fossil fuels also pollutes the air. For example, many farm machines run on gasoline or diesel fuel, both of which are made from oil. When burned, these fuels release smoke into the air that can harm plants and animals.

Tomatoes on a farm

A worker checks bottles of ketchup before they are sent to a supermarket.

Food production requires about 10 percent of all the energy used in the United States.

Ketchup and other products are delivered to supermarkets by trucks.

Eating Green

More and more people are trying to reduce the amount of fossil fuels used to produce food by **eating green**. These people are choosing to buy foods grown in ways that use as little energy as possible and that don't pollute the environment.

This way of eating isn't easy. Most fruits and vegetables in supermarkets are grown on giant **industrial farms** that use lots of energy to grow and harvest crops. These farms also use **chemical fertilizers** to help the plants grow and **pesticides** to keep insects from eating them. These products are made in factories that use huge amounts of energy.

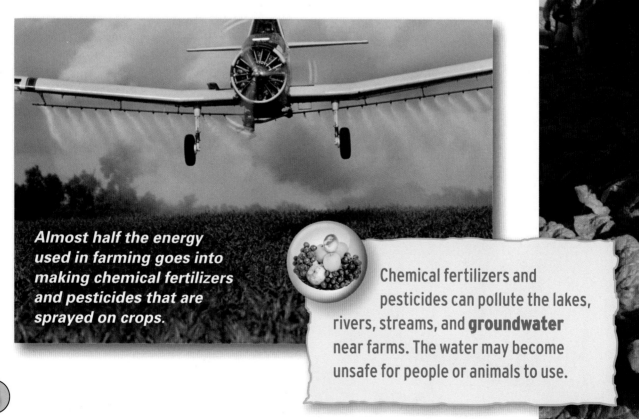

Almost half the energy used in farming goes into making chemical fertilizers and pesticides that are sprayed on crops.

Chemical fertilizers and pesticides can pollute the lakes, rivers, streams, and **groundwater** near farms. The water may become unsafe for people or animals to use.

Today, three-fourths of all the food sold in the United States comes from industrial farms such as this one.

A Long Journey

Once vegetables and fruits leave industrial farms, they often travel long distances to stores. For example, people in Virginia may eat potatoes grown in Idaho, which means the food traveled about 2,000 miles (3,219 km)!

Shipping food a long way requires a lot of energy. Trucks, for example, run on gasoline. When they transport food hundreds or thousands of miles (km), a lot of gasoline is burned. This sends **greenhouse gases** into the air, which trap heat inside Earth's **atmosphere**. Many scientists think that greenhouse gases are slowly raising the world's air and water temperatures to dangerously high levels. This type of worldwide heating is called **global warming**.

Many of the trucks that carry food have large refrigerators to keep their cargo fresh. Energy is needed to power the refrigerators.

Fruits and vegetables shipped long distances are often picked before they are ripe, so they won't spoil during their journey. As a result, they may have fewer nutrients than produce picked at the peak of ripeness.

Where Most of the Fresh Vegetables in the United States Come From

CANADA

California's Central Valley

UNITED STATES

Pacific Ocean

Atlantic Ocean

MEXICO

N W E S

About 90 percent of all the fresh vegetables eaten in the United States are grown in California's Central Valley.

Local and Seasonal

If most foods are shipped long distances, using lots of energy, how can people eat green? One way is to buy fruits and vegetables that are grown **locally**. These foods travel very short distances from small farms to the market.

Locally grown foods can often be found at **farmers markets**. The fruits and vegetables sold there are usually picked just when they have turned ripe, so they are *in season*. Tomatoes, for example, are in season from about July to October in the United States. That's the time when they are ready to be picked from the plants, taste freshest, and have the most nutrients.

Farmers markets like this one in California are great places to buy local foods that are in season.

Many small-farm owners set up roadside stands where they sell their freshly picked fruits and vegetables.

FRESH PICKED
LOCAL
FARM

More Americans are buying locally grown food. In 2008, there were about 4,600 farmers markets in the United States, up from 1,700 in 1994.

Factory Foods

People who want to eat green also need to cut back on foods **processed** in factories. The processing requires lots of energy, and then more energy is needed to package the finished product. In addition, natural resources that are in limited supply are used to make the packaging that holds the food. For example, oil is used to make plastic bottles, and many metal cans are made from iron. Once the food is eaten, the package it comes in ends up as garbage. Sometimes the package is **recycled**. However, more often than not, it is buried in a **landfill**.

Factory foods can be unhealthy, too. Chemicals called **preservatives** are often added to foods to keep them from spoiling during travel. For example, sodium—a chemical found in salt—is used in large amounts in many canned goods. While some sodium is needed for the body to function properly, too much isn't good for a person's health.

Much of the food Americans eat is packaged in factories.

Empty food boxes and containers become garbage that often ends up in landfills.

Only about one-third of all the garbage in the United States gets recycled.

Buying Organic

Green eaters want food that is produced in a way that doesn't harm the environment. That's why many green shoppers buy fruits and vegetables grown on **organic** farms. These farms use fewer machines than industrial farms and don't use chemical fertilizers and pesticides. Also, **artificial** preservatives are not added to the foods before shipping.

Although organic foods are healthful, they aren't always easy to find. In the United States, most produce comes from industrial farms. However, as organic foods become more popular, the number of organic farms in America is increasing.

Organic fruits and vegetables sometimes don't look very pretty. They may be misshapen or have spots or holes. However, many people believe that they taste better than nonorganic foods.

There are more than 700,000 organic farms in 130 countries around the world, such as this one in Shanghai, China.

An organic farm uses about 30 percent less energy than a regular farm of the same size.

How Much Meat?

Many green eaters buy little or no meat for several reasons. First, producing meat uses a lot of fossil fuels. Cows and pigs, for example, eat large amounts of grain. Lots of fuel is burned up by the machines that are needed to grow it. Second, packaging the meat for the market and keeping it frozen or refrigerated requires even more energy. Finally, trucks usually travel long distances to get the meat to stores. That's a lot of fossil fuels being burned!

Some green eaters wonder if eating meat is even healthy. Large meat producers often crowd their animals together. For example, thousands of cows are sometimes jammed into a single **feedlot**, which causes some animals to get sick. So to prevent diseases they're given medicines. Often, they're also given chemicals to help them grow big quickly. Sometimes these medicines and chemicals can remain in the meat even after the animals are killed. This means that people might be eating them, too.

Cows eating grain in a feedlot

It takes about 16 pounds (7,258 g) of grain to produce one pound (454 g) of hamburger meat.

Raising Better Animals

People can eat green and still enjoy meat. How? Some farmers and ranchers raise animals in ways that don't harm the environment. For example, some growers allow cows to wander in fields instead of keeping them in crowded feedlots. This **free-range** lifestyle saves on energy because machines aren't needed to bring grain to numerous feedlots. Instead, the grain is placed in a central location that the cows walk to when they're hungry. Animals that roam free are also less likely to get sick than enclosed animals.

Some farmers and ranchers also produce organic meat. They feed their animals only organic grain, which is grown without pesticides and chemical fertilizers. Many people think that this makes the meat healthier for humans to eat.

Organic beef can be found in supermarkets.

Some green eaters don't eat the meat or eggs of chickens because few chickens are given a free-range lifestyle. Most egg-laying chickens are kept in a caged space about half as long as a piece of notebook paper.

Caged egg-laying chickens

Grass-Fed and Green

What's better than a free-range cow? A grass-fed cow! Grass-fed cattle are allowed to eat the grasses that naturally grow in pastures and meadows. Many people think their meat tastes even better than the meat of free-range cows that are fed grain.

Grass-fed animals also help the environment. By wandering around pastures, they spread their manure—or body waste—over a large area. The manure is a natural fertilizer that helps grass grow. By contrast, feedlot manure must be gathered up and carried away by trucks. The trucks burn gasoline and use up more energy.

Grass-fed cows eat straight from the ground. Little energy is spent in growing their food.

Manure that is hauled away in trucks is often dumped in lagoons or lakes, which can sometimes cause water pollution.

Cow manure being pumped into a lagoon

Food for Thought

Eating green is a great idea because it helps both people and the environment. When shoppers buy locally grown meat and produce, they are supporting farmers in their area and buying foods that were not shipped long distances. They may also be eating more healthfully. Compared with factory-processed foods, fresh foods usually contain more nutrients.

For most people, the first step to eating green is simply learning about the foods they buy and where they come from. People should aim to buy foods that are made using less energy. Over time, green eaters will almost certainly help improve the environment, as well as their own good health.

Despite all the food produced around the world, many poor people still go hungry. There are nearly one billion people who don't get enough to eat.

Twenty percent of all the oil burned in the United States is used to produce food.

Grow a Vegetable Garden

Growing your own vegetables is a big step toward greener eating. Here are some of the benefits:

- It's cheaper. Growing your own lettuce and tomatoes is almost always less expensive than buying them in a store.

- It's healthier. Vegetables from your own yard can be eaten the same day they are picked, before they lose any nutrients.

- It saves energy. Home-grown vegetables don't need to be delivered by truck, so they don't contribute to environmental pollution.

- It's safer. By growing your own vegetables, you can avoid using pesticides and chemical fertilizers.

- The food tastes better. Vegetables can be picked when they are perfectly ripe, which is when they taste best.

Growing vegetables can be a fun experience.

Start Composting

Composting is a process where garbage is allowed to rot, or **decompose**, and then is added to the soil. This makes the soil richer in nutrients. Composting is great for the environment. Here's why:

- Cut grass, leaves, and food wastes such as apple cores and banana peels make up almost one-quarter of all household garbage. Composting these items reduces the amount of garbage that must be bagged and sent to landfills.

- Composting in a garden can help keep some plants free of pests and disease. Composted soil acts like a natural pesticide, and in some cases it can eliminate the need for chemical pesticides.

This boy adds grass clippings to a compost pile.

What to Compost

Create a compost pile in your yard. Put in these items:

- fruit and vegetable wastes, nutshells
- clean paper, shredded newspaper, clean cardboard
- eggshells, coffee grounds, tea bags
- cut grass, leaves, sawdust, wood chips
- cotton and wool rags
- hair and lint from clothes dryers and vacuum cleaners

This waste is perfect for a compost pile.

Fair Trade

One way to support greener eating is by buying Fair Trade foods. These foods are grown in ways that don't harm the environment. The Fair Trade certification also means the farmers who grew the food were paid a fair wage for their work. Popular Fair Trade items include coffee, tea, cocoa, chocolate, fruit, sugar, and rice. They are sold at more than 35,000 stores in the United States.

Remember the following when you are in a food store:

- All Fair Trade products carry a Fair Trade Certified label. Look for the label when you shop.
- Buying Fair Trade food helps poor farmers, who often live in **developing countries**. They are paid more to grow Fair Trade products than they would be paid for non–Fair Trade items.

Workers on Fair Trade farms, such as this coffee farm in Haiti, usually have better working conditions than do other farm workers in developing countries.

Shopping for Greener Food

One way to buy green food is to go to a farmers market. If you can't get to one, you can still buy green foods at the supermarket. When shopping, look for foods that carry these labels or words:

- **USDA Organic**—This means that the U.S. government has checked to make sure that everything in the food is completely organic.

- **Organic**—This label means that at least 95 percent of the food's ingredients are organic.

- **Made with Organic Ingredients**—Foods with this label must contain at least 70 percent organic ingredients.

- **Free Range**—This label on meat means that it comes from animals that were allowed to roam freely, though it may have been for as little as five minutes a day.

Dining Out

If you choose a restaurant, try to dine at those that support green eating. Some restaurants state on their menus that they serve organic, free range, or Fair Trade foods. When in doubt, ask a person on the waitstaff, the chef, or the restaurant owner.

You can check for green restaurants in your neighborhood by visiting the Green Restaurant Association website: **www.dinegreen.com**. Restaurants listed on this website try to get their foods from places that work to help the environment. The restaurants also practice recycling.

Restaurants that have this Green Restaurant Association seal have to meet special guidelines and requirements.

Which Fish?

Food experts argue about the value of fish in a green diet. Some think it's important to eat, while others do not. Yet everyone agrees that certain fish are healthier than others. Much depends on where the fish come from. To find the types of fish that are best to eat where you live, visit www.montereybayaquarium.org/cr/cr_seafoodwatch/download.aspx.

Not all fish live and are caught in the wild. Some are raised on fish farms—places where large numbers of fish are grown together in tanks and other enclosed areas.

Before you eat farm-raised fish, consider these facts:

- Certain types of farmed fish can have high levels of chemicals that were added to the water. The chemicals may harm people who eat the fish.

- Different kinds of farmed fish, like fenced-in cattle, often get sick due to crowded living conditions. They are given medicine that may stay in their bodies even after they become human food.

- Some fish farms use pesticides to keep bugs off the fish.

Most of the salmon that Americans eat is raised on fish farms.

Everyone needs to get involved in eating green. Here are some things that you can do:

- Grow your own vegetable garden. Look in a gardening book or online for information on how to plant one.

- Start composting. Use the information on page 25 to help you get started.

- Convince your family to shop as much as possible at a farmers market. Look online to find farmers markets near you.

- Ask grocers and farmers about the foods you buy. If you don't see organic items in your grocery store, ask for them. Often, grocers will order products that their customers request.

- Try to eat more fresh food and less factory-processed food. Most fresh foods have few or no preservatives and are healthier for people than processed items.

- Pay attention to food labels when you shop. Look for those that tell you the food was produced in a way that doesn't harm the environment. Use the information on page 27 to help you.

Learn More Online

To learn more about eating green, visit
www.bearportpublishing.com/GoingGreen

Glossary

artificial (ar-ti-FISH-uhl) not natural; made by humans

atmosphere (AT-muhss-fihr) the mixture of gases that surrounds Earth

chemical fertilizers (KEM-uh-kuhl FUR-tuh-*lize*-urz) plant food that is made from chemicals

decompose (dee-kuhm-POHZ) to rot or break down into another form

developing countries (di-VEL-uhp-ing KUHN-treez) countries in which there are not many industries and many of the people are poor

eating green (EET-ing GREEN) buying and eating foods that are produced with little energy and few chemicals in order to keep the planet clean

energy (EN-ur-jee) power from different sources that makes things work or produces heat

farmers markets (FAR-murz MAR-kits) places where farmers bring their goods to sell

feedlot (FEED-lot) a large, fenced-in area where animals are crowded together and fed grain

fossil fuels (FOSS-uhl FYOO-uhlz) energy sources such as gas, oil, and coal that are formed from the remains of animals and plants that died millions of years ago

free-range (FREE-raynj) allowed to wander about; not kept in small, fenced-in areas

global warming (GLOHB-uhl WORM-ing) the gradual heating up of Earth caused by a buildup of greenhouse gases that trap heat from the sun in Earth's atmosphere

greenhouse gases (GREEN-houss GAS-iz) gases such as carbon dioxide and methane that trap warm air in Earth's atmosphere so it cannot escape into space; the gases responsible for global warming

groundwater (GROUND-waw-tur) water located belowground

industrial farms (in-DUHSS-tree-uhl FARMZ) large farms that are run like factories

landfill (LAND-fill) a large hole in the ground that serves as a dumping spot for garbage

locally (LOH-kuh-lee) in the area where people live

organic (or-GAN-ik) grown without using chemical fertilizers or pesticides

pesticides (PESS-tuh-sidez) chemicals that kill insects and other pests that damage crops

preservatives (pri-ZUR-vuh-tivz) chemicals put into foods to keep them from spoiling

processed (PROSS-esst) treated in a way to make it last longer and easier to ship

recycled (ree-SYE-kuhld) to turn used, unwanted materials into something useful

sustainable (suh-STAYN-uh-buhl) a way of living that does not use up nonrenewable resources; living in a way that can be continued forever

Index

Bibliography

Langley, Andrew. *Is Organic Food Better? (What do You Think?)*. Chicago: Heinemann (2008).

Robinson, Jo. *Pasture Perfect: The Far-Reaching Benefits of Choosing Meat, Eggs, and Dairy Products from Grass-Fed Animals*. Vashon, WA: Vashon Island Press (2004).

Read More

Claybourne, Anna. *Composting: Decomposition (Do It Yourself)*. Chicago: Heinemann Educational Books (2008).

Leavitt, Amie Jane. *A Backyard Vegetable Garden for Kids*. Hockessin, DE: Mitchell Lane Publishers (2008).

About the Author

Sunita Apte has always been passionate about cooking and all things related to food. She has written over 40 books for children and teens. She lives in Brooklyn, New York.